This Journal Belongs To:

Name ....

Email ....

Telephone ....

Breathe

Wellbeing

JOURNAL

AMMONITE
PRESS

Wellbeing

It's something that everyone deserves a sense of, and this journal is here to help you discover yours. Finding time for yourself in today's fast-paced world can often feel unachievable. Rushing from one task to another, prioritising everyone else's needs above your own, struggling to fit in regular exercise, even a good night's sleep. But it doesn't have to be this way. Here at *Breathe*, the original mindfulness magazine, we've discovered the secret to reclaiming your life is to start small. Just a few simple, gradual changes can make the world of difference.

And this journal is filled with ways to help you do just that. A curated collection of our articles mixed with brand new easy exercises, think of it as a field guide to wellbeing – a companion to carry with you and dip into, wherever you are. Discover rituals to soothe and nourish, practical ideas to declutter and get organised, tips on how to slow down and calm those racing thoughts. Beautifully illustrated, with space to record your innermost thoughts and ideas, use it to take those first rejuvenating steps towards a more relaxed, more fulfilled you.

Breathe

breathemagazine.com

Contents

In search of balance

Sometimes the day's chores can seem overwhelming, but there are ways to create a fresh rhythm to life that has room for work, play and downtime

The busier life becomes the harder it is to stay on top of everything. The more you do, the faster your stress levels rise. Even multitasking is a downward spiral. According to experts, each time you switch tasks it can take up to five minutes to refocus, and the very act of toggling between tasks raises cortisol levels. And so turns the never-ending circle – not dissimilar to a hamster's wheel.

It is time to get off the wheel, take a deep breath and restore the balance in your life. And to do this you will need to develop a new set of rules or rituals. These create a different lifestyle rhythm that once learned will never be forgotten. Balance is about equality, about weighing up the good with the bad. It is about not getting lost in perfection and, perhaps even more so, about accepting imperfection.

1 Get up earlier

In his book, *The Miracle Morning*, Hal Elrod suggests getting up super early before anyone else is awake. In the quiet stillness of the early hours you can plough through tasks that would be difficult to manage during a normal day. Start with small steps – set the alarm just 15 minutes earlier and use that time to do something that will help you focus on the day ahead. Maybe meditate for a few minutes: practise a one-minute ritual to help you stop, inhale and reset.

2 Plan ahead

This can be helpful in staying productive and organised, especially when trying to fit new things into a schedule. Willpower is a finite resource – people only have a set amount of it each day – so try not to waste it on trivial rather than important decisions. If you plan ahead, simple things like meals for the week, it takes away the need for willpower or decision-making and your resources are available for other things, like being creative or concentrating on goals.

3 Give yourself 'grey time'

Each day tends to begin with a plan. Within it there are different blocks of time: meetings, the day's jobs or tasks, and grey time. The latter is important to stay aligned – it's a space to think and review. Remember to plan it into the diary however relentless your schedule.

4 Say no

You can say no. So many people agree to do things, even pretend they would love to, when inside they're secretly wondering how to fit everything in. There are only 24 hours in the day – and some of those need to be spent taking care of yourself. It is perfectly normal to feel guilty about saying no, so offer an alternative instead: 'I can't do that, but I could do this.' Soften the blow by saying no in a pleasant way: 'Thank you so much for thinking of me. It sounds like a great idea, but at the moment I'm pretty overstretched. Do keep me in mind for next time.' Any guilt felt at the time will quickly be replaced by a wave of relief and empowerment.

5 Edit your to-do list – and be ruthless

How many of the things on your list really need to be done? What can you delegate or outsource? Cut down the to-do list to two or three things a day. When the to-do list is short, it's easier to feel more positive about reaching the end, so you are able to get more done. It sounds counterintuitive, and it is, but it works.

6 Have a clear-out

Tackle that neglected drawer, empty the in-box and start afresh, donate old belongings to charity. Whatever you decide to do, it is important. It will give a sense of accomplishment and make you feel empowered to tackle other tasks. And you will have more 'breathing space' to help create balance.

7 Think positive

Choose not to be negative, not to look backwards, not to let petty things get you down, and only think about positive outcomes and solutions. This way you won't waste energy on negative factors.

8 Be kind to yourself

Rather than think about the things you could have done better, get into the habit of celebrating what you have done well. It is important to reward yourself for your achievements, large and small. And remember these high points when things go wrong – as they invariably do. You are what you choose to be in life.

Things I've done that deserve celebrating

....

....

....

....

....

....

....

....

....

....

....

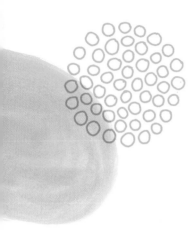

Slowly does it

From food to work to holidays, the evidence that taking life down a notch is beneficial to happiness is growing

The concept of slow living began back in the 1980s with the slow food movement. Originally the word slow wasn't used for its literal meaning but as an acronym for sustainable, local, organic and whole. The slow food movement still has its focus on growing, rearing and consuming food in a way that's good for the planet, for humans and for all living beings. In recent years, slow living has also become an all-encompassing approach to life rather than just one area of it.

As a term, slow living is quite broad and open to individual interpretation. It doesn't necessarily mean living life at half-speed compared to the rest of the population, but it does embrace a more considered, thoughtful approach to how you live; which, in turn, can result in a less frenetic pace of life.

While the world becomes more digitised and reliance on technology increases, slow living is a move towards a more analogue way of being. It doesn't mean ditching your smartphone or laptop, but taking a more mindful attitude towards how you use them.

Stepping off

Essentially, the movement is about letting go of the need to be busy, to be always moving on to the next task, to be trying to do and have everything, and instead being purposeful in what you do, paying attention to what's happening now and experiencing life as it is. There can be a lot of self-expectation as well as the feeling that you have to live up to a certain ideal for others – slow living suggests you drop those pressures. By being mindful of how you compare yourself to other people, the standards to which you hold yourself, and how you honour your boundaries, you can recognise when life has become a treadmill that you want to step off. Slow living is the antidote to life on auto-pilot.

At the heart of the movement is connection. It can be this feeling of connectedness to other people and to your own life that is lost when you live at top speed. When the calendar is full of meetings, events and after-school activities, when your work days are getting longer, when you find it difficult to say no or to admit you need help, when there are apps and box-sets to occupy any spare time and virtual Joneses in social media as well as those in real life to keep up with, you can feel disconnected from your life – as it's taken on a momentum of its own and you're carried along with little say in the matter.

Slow living suggests that you hop off the merry-go-round to see how else you could go about your life: to find out if your current timetable is providing you with the quality of life you want. It may be that some aspects would benefit from being taken down a notch or two, while there are other areas where you're happy with the pace and feel no need to change. Considering how connected you feel to your partner, children, friends, family, even yourself, can help you work out if you would benefit from a little more slow living.

Ask yourself...

What in your life makes you feel busy?

....

....

....

....

....

....

When did you last feel connected to those around you?

....

....

....

....

....

Is anything stopping you from slowing down right now?

....

....

....

....

....

How would life be different if you were able to slow down more?

....

....

....

....

....

Ways to go slow

*Everyday ideas for living a more connected
and conscious lifestyle*

1 Slow technology
Loosen your grip on your digital devices by taking steps to spend less time
on screen. Leave your phone at home when you go for a walk, have a digital
device curfew, or collect social media apps into a folder on your last home
screen to make scrolling through the apps less automatic.

2 Slow food
If food shopping and preparation is a source of stress, reconnect with the
food you eat by growing some yourself, even just one ingredient. With
minimal space and time you can grow salad leaves, herbs or tomatoes. If
preparing meals from scratch feels too daunting, try one dish for starters.

3 Slow home
Having a home full of stuff can create an oppressive air and literally slow you
down as it takes longer to wade through drawers, shelves and cupboards to
find what you're looking for. Take one room or item type at a time and have
a clear-out. Whatever doesn't have a use or you don't love can go to charity,
be recycled or put into the bin, or be sold.

4 Slow travel
Trying to get to where you need to be as quickly as possible can mean
you're missing out on the hidden treasures of unexplored routes. Leave
the car at home and take a walk, ride a bike or travel on public transport
to get to your destination, where practical. Make the extra journey time
part of the experience and look for what you might have been missing
from your driver's seat.

5 Slow activities
Find satisfaction in a creative pursuit, such as drawing, paper cutting,
origami, crocheting, model building or simply reading a book that asks
you to slow down and take your time. Take a stroll through a local park or
woodland and notice the colours of the flowers, the insects living around
them, the different species of trees, the sun (or rain) coming through the
canopy, the sound of birdsong and the smell of nature.

6 Slow days

Clear a weekend of plans and do what takes your fancy when you wake up. Check the weather forecast, see how you feel and consider what you don't usually get to do because you've already made plans. Resist any urge to fill the time with chores and instead think about what you could do just for the joy of it. Perhaps that's taking a picnic to the local park, playing a board game, watching a classic movie, baking a cake or exploring an unknown area of your neighbourhood.

7 Slow family

Create times in the day and week when you connect with each other as a family. Eat dinner together at the table, greet and leave each other in person with hugs rather than yelling hellos and goodbyes, or take part in a family activity or sport.

8 Slow together

Gather together a handful of friends to share a meal and a few relaxed hours. Keep the food simple, perhaps suggest everyone brings a pot-luck dish, and don't stress about how pristine your home is. The focus is on spending time talking to people you care about and enjoy being with, rather than where you are, how much the wine costs or the complexity of the menu.

9 Slow holidays

Consider how you can best make use of taking time away from everyday life to recharge. The urge can be to include as many experiences as possible and, while this may be enjoyable, you can also return home feeling the need for a rest. Schedule time to sit and people watch, to reflect on where you visited or what you did each day, or just stay in one place and take a slower mode of transport.

10 Slow moments

Even in the middle of a hectic day you can take a slow living moment. Focus your attention on your breath and where you feel it most clearly – in your abdomen, chest, nose – for a few breaths. Then scan your body from your feet to your head, noticing how it feels without judging or changing it. Move your attention slowly to take in what you can hear, what you can smell and what you can see. Come back to your breath for a few seconds more and then carry on with your day. Know that any time you feel the need, you can bring your attention back to your breath for a few moments of calm.

home
sweet
home

Make yourself right at home

'Home is where the heart is' – a place filled with the people and possessions you love. But too often people hold on to stuff they don't need, use or cherish. So how do you declutter, enrich your life and turn bricks and mortar into your own personal haven?

For many, the phrase 'mindful home' will conjure up images of a spiritual space – ornaments of Buddhist monks, everything perfectly placed Feng Shui-style and just the right balance of yin and yang.

For most people, though – with time, money and patience for household jobs in short supply – the reality is that this picture-perfect image doesn't exist. More likely, it is a place of organised chaos, with a feeling that you're running just to stand still. So how do you go about creating a harmonious abode?

Reflection of the inner self

It's not so much what's on the surface that counts, it's what resides within, or at the heart of, the shell. It's about what your home embodies and says about you. After all, it's a space you shape and mould to express your individual personality, interests and lifestyle – almost like an extension of you – somewhere you can truly be yourself and project how you want to be seen to others.

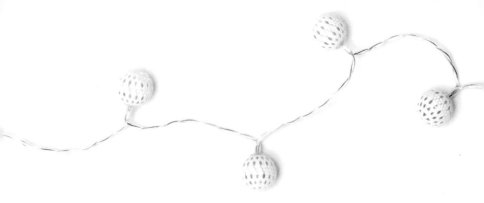

Look with fresh eyes

As somewhere you spend most of your life, you can sometimes be too close to your home to be able to reflect on what it says about you. Try imagining yourself as a visitor to your house for the first time. It can be a useful way to gain fresh perspective and consider, without judgement, what it says about you.

What would you change to make it the home you desire?

....

....

....

....

The mindful clear-out

While you're reflecting on any possible changes, look around you: might it be time for a declutter? It's truly remarkable how much people hoard, often without even realising it. This is why a good, old-fashioned spring clean from time to time is so important. So let's get stuck in. To make sure you don't lose motivation, imagine what it would be like to have a clutter-free home and ask yourself why you would like to live this way. Writing a mission statement, including the benefits of an uncluttered life, can be a great motivational tool to look back on, and will help to keep you focused.

Reasons to live a clutter-free life

....

....

....

....

One thing at a time

Decluttering can seem like a mammoth task. Instead of looking at your home in its entirety, break it down into rooms or, even better, focus on one category at a time, such as clothes, books or stationery. It's much less daunting and quicker to get results this way. Making a list of what you want to get done can help to maintain focus and momentum, plus there's something ever so satisfying in being able to tick them off one by one.

Tasks to complete

▶ ....
....
....

▶ ....
....
....

▶ ....
....
....

▶ ....
....
....

▶ ....
....
....

▶ ....
....
....

Space to breathe

The first job is discarding items. Going through your belongings with full awareness gives you the chance to consider whether you actually need, use or cherish each item you come across. It can be hard to let go of some things as they might invoke memories of the past, but this is where you must remember you are living in the present. Sometimes you have to be cruel to be kind. Instead of throwing your items straight in the bin, you can soften the blow by putting them into a bag for the charity shop, letting others get joy from them and contributing to a worthy cause at the same time.

Once you have discarded the items, apart from feeling psychologically lighter and clearer, you will be able to see what you're left with and neatly organise them back into place. This allows you to become fully aware and appreciate all the things that make up the home you love.

Keep it under control

Post declutter-fest, having freed up all that extra space, you might be tempted to treat yourself to a little spending spree. Are you one of those people who can go into complete shopaholic mode and rush out into the sales, buying things for no reason other than that you consider them a bargain? To stop yourself from accumulating more stuff, try to take a breather and check whether you need, or even truly desire, a so-called bargain. Ask yourself: 'Am I buying this item for the sake of buying it or is it going to add to my life in some way?' It's a useful tactic to try when you next hit the shops.

Things you need to buy

....

....

....

....

....

....

Clean like a monk

Keeping your home in shipshape condition doesn't need to be a drag. In Zen temples, monks are assigned to carry out a specific cleaning task every day for 20 minutes. They fully immerse themselves silently in the job, and once the time is up they stop working – whether they have completed it or not – and continue with their day. This practice is called 'soji' and has been replicated in Japanese schools, where children carry out 20 minutes of cleaning as part of their daily routine.

Sticking with the mindset that every job you start needs to be finished can result in putting chores off until you know you have time to get them done. But by cleaning like a monk, your focus shifts from finishing the task to doing it, so you're able to get household jobs done over the week without overcomplicating everything. What's more, it can help you to do the mundane chores even if you don't want to do them; to receive and accept them without preference, resistance or protest. If Japanese children can manage 20 minutes, so can you.

Why not give this a go? Next time you carry out your chores, stay focused and try not to be distracted by thoughts other than the task at hand, ensuring the 20 minutes are as productive as they can be and you're not cheating yourself.

If you start to lose focus, drifting in and out of thoughts, merely observe and acknowledge their presence, notice their content and consciously choose to bring your attention back to what you're doing. With a set time to work in, it's easy to get distracted by clock-watching. You could get around this by setting an alarm on your phone. It doesn't have to be 20 minutes: choose an amount of time that suits you and your lifestyle.

Time out at home

There's nothing like a day spent at home, but busy lives mean these times are few and far between. Your home becomes a crash pad for sleeping. Any chance you do get to sit down and appreciate the home you've made is often interrupted by cold calls, a neighbour unexpectedly popping by for a chat or the daunting to-do list hanging over your head. So, what's the answer? A mindful home retreat is a great way to enjoy the comforts of your own space and enjoy some respite. There's no need to book a weekend break abroad for some time out. You can save those pennies and opt for a true staycation.

Clear your afternoon of any commitments and switch off your phone so that you won't be disturbed, and try spending the time carrying out three mindful activities. You could tap into your creative side by painting for an hour or two; read a book you've been meaning to finish; or prepare some nourishing home cooking. Carrying out each one with full awareness will allow your body and mind to enjoy each moment as it passes.

Mindful activities you'd like to try

....

....

....

....

....

....

....

....

....

....

And finally...

Take time to observe and appreciate fully the haven you've made, tucked away from the hustle and bustle of the world outside. The place you miss when you're away and to which you look forward to returning. The space you can forever adapt to reflect who you are, where you are in your life and how you want to live. At the end of the day, there really is no place like home.

Create your own mental health first aid kit

When you suffer a cut or a graze you reach for the plasters, but what do you do when you're feeling frazzled? Here's what to put aside to soothe your mind and nerves on those off-days

Most households have a first aid kit of some sort. A tin or Tupperware box with plasters, creams and painkillers, or a drawer that's home to these plus a host of random bits and bobs. But what if you're feeling bruised and battered by life, with no external scars to show for it? Where do you turn to soothe the pain then?

While a traditional first aid kit treats your physical ailments, the contents aren't that helpful when you're suffering mental anguish. Plasters and bandages won't slow the stream of anxious thoughts running around your head or lift your spirits. This is where another type of first aid kit is needed. A mental health first aid kit can be more personalised to your individual needs than a standard one, and it can include a wide variety of items, both tangible and digital.

Your kit can live in a box in your house, in a pouch in your handbag or it can be spread all over the place – position it wherever it's likely to be useful. What's important is that your kit will provide you with what you need, when you need it.

So what do you include in your mental health first aid kit?
Here are a few ideas to get you started...

Your smartphone

The advantage of using your phone as part of your kit is that it's the one item you're likely to have with you wherever you are. Create a folder of meditation apps, so if you need to take a few minutes to calm your mind or nerves you can listen to a guided meditation. There are also apps that prompt you to think about what you're thankful for.

Most phones have a voice memo app where you can record yourself talking. Perhaps make a message to play to yourself when you're feeling particularly anxious, upset or low. Or use the countless photos on your phone and put together a digital album that makes you smile. It could include photos of your family, friends and beloved pets, occasions that remind you of happy memories or scenes that uplift you.

Why not put together a playlist of favourite tunes that lift your spirits, improve your mood and energise you, or compile a selection that feels soothing and restful, in case that's what helps at a particular moment. What songs could you include?

Your comfort playlist

....

....

....

....

....

....

....

....

....

....

....

Essential oils

Essential oils can be a speedy solution because when you inhale the scent it goes straight to your limbic system, which affects your emotion and memory. That's why sometimes all it takes is a whiff of a smell to instantly change your mood and bring back memories. Keep a little bottle handy to inhale when required.

Choose your scent

- Grounding oils, such as cedarwood and frankincense, can help you to feel stronger and more comfortable in your own skin, nurturing self-confidence and self-esteem.

- Citrus oils, like grapefruit and orange, are naturally uplifting, boosting general mood and positivity, leaving you feeling happier about yourself.

- Clary, sage and rosemary promote mental clarity, reducing negative mental chatter and leading to a stronger sense of purpose, focus and action. This can help with confident decision-making.

NOW TRY THIS EXERCISE...

- Sitting comfortably, dab aromatherapy balm onto your pulse points and inhale.

- Take long, deep breaths right into your belly and exhale slowly. Notice the belly rising and falling with every breath, and then just count your breath – one in, two out, three in and so on until you reach 20.

Note how it makes you feel

Quick fixes

When you're struggling mentally, a list of actions that you can choose from to help yourself can be useful. Write them down here so you can access them easily as and when you need them.

   What you write on the list is personal to you. What would make you feel better when you're having a tough day? Maybe going for a walk, listening to your comfort playlist or phoning a friend, or more restful suggestions like taking a nap, reading a chapter of your book or meditating.

   It's worth noting down some basic ideas too – drinking a glass of water, making a cup of tea, eating something nourishing or taking a few deep breaths in and out may seem obvious, but it's easy to forget the importance of such simple actions to wellbeing.

Your action list

....

....

....

....

....

....

....

....

....

....

....

....

....

....

....

....

....

Journal and pen

There could be any number of reasons why you feel the need to dive into your mental health first aid kit, but whatever's going on inside your head, taking it out of your brain and putting it down on paper can help. Whether that's as a stream of consciousness, a to-do list of everything you're trying to remember or reasons for and against an argument, writing it here in this journal can ease the burden.

Focusing on the good things around you can also be useful. Take a few minutes to jot down what you appreciate in your life, what you feel grateful for and what makes you smile. This enables your brain to think of the positives rather than the negatives (it can't do both at once), giving you a break from stress. And having them written down means that on another occasion you can flick back and recall positive moments.

Whatever else you choose to add to your kit – a quotation you find inspiring, a nourishing snack, something to read or even a puzzle – remember you can add to it or swap things in and out depending on how you feel and what you need at the time. What matters is that you now have something to make those stressful situations that little bit easier.

Wide awake – and worried

Lying awake in the small hours, with anxious thoughts seemingly your only company, is no fun. Here's how to put them in their place and get some precious sleep

Picture the scene. You've woken up in the middle of the night or early morning. The rest of the house is quiet, it's dark and your mind has leapt into action with thoughts and worries spinning around at high speed. You don't want to be awake, you don't want to have these thoughts, you feel alone and your own mind is driving you crazy. You just want your brain to stop, you're tired, anxious and you want to be asleep.

Sound familiar? It's not fun. Having strategies to call upon when you wake up worrying in the small hours means that not only can you help yourself but it also gives you the confidence that you can deal with your whirring brain – and that makes a big difference. So, let's see what can be done about it.

Know that you're not alone

When you're lying there in the quiet darkness with thoughts reverberating loudly around your mind, it's easy to feel isolated. Even with a house full of people it can still feel like you're the only person in the world awake with a head full of worry. But know this: you're not alone. There's a good chance that in homes up and down the land there are other people lying awake at the exact same time you are, also wishing their brains would shush, that the thought ticker tape would stop, willing themselves to sleep.

Give yourself compassion

When you're exhausted and have a busy day ahead you can feel frustrated that your brain isn't letting you sleep – that it's insisting on thinking loudly when you need to rest. So you get annoyed with yourself, you tell yourself to relax, you push away the unwanted thoughts, willing yourself to stop being so difficult and to just turn over and sleep. That doesn't work so well, though, does it? Forcing your mind to go blank, squeezing your eyes shut and burrowing under the duvet is unlikely to do the trick, however much you want it to. So stop trying.

Recognise this is difficult. Tell yourself that tossing and turning with a runaway train of thoughts when you want to be asleep is hard and it's understandable you're stressed. Imagine it's a good friend lying awake feeling this way and think how you would talk to her. Acknowledging how you're feeling and practising self-compassion has been shown to be a more effective calming technique than mentally beating yourself up.

Focus on a mantra

Here's a mantra you can repeat to yourself to soothe a stressed mind:

'This feels really difficult right now. Everyone feels like this sometimes. I will give myself the kindness I need'

Try repeating this mantra to yourself, or adapt it so it feels right for you, and see how it makes you feel. It can be used in any challenging situation so it's a good one to have stored up, ready to repeat when needed.

It isn't a magic bullet, you won't say these words and immediately fall asleep. But you are making it easier to calm down so you can get to a point where you drop off again. If willing yourself to sleep isn't working, give self-compassion a go instead.

Acknowledge what you're thinking

Worrying or frightening thoughts are not something to which you want to give attention. But if you try hard not to think of a giraffe in leg warmers all you can think about is a giraffe in leg warmers. So, it might feel uncomfortable, but acknowledge what you're thinking about. There's no need to look at whether your thoughts are right or wrong. And it doesn't matter what you're anxious about because you're not addressing the worries. Getting involved in your thoughts in the middle of the night isn't going to resolve them.

Instead, simply acknowledge the fear and the worry: 'I know I'm worried about x.' Give yourself compassion: 'It's really hard for me to have this going round in my head right now.' And recognise that at this exact moment there is no action you can take so let it go: 'Right now it's the middle of the night, I'm in bed, there's nothing I can do to address these worries, so I will no longer give them my attention.'

You can even give yourself a specific time when you will face the worries, such as later that morning at 11am. Some people find writing worries down can help to clear the mind.

Worries to address later

....

....

....

....

....

....

....

....

....

....

....

....

....

Mindful body scan

Give this exercise a go next time you're having trouble sleeping

Focus your attention on each body part, starting with your toes and travelling slowly all the way up to the top of your head, noticing what's touching the mattress and what isn't. You're not trying to change or judge anything, you're just taking time to give all your concentration to each bit of your body.

Start with your feet. Are some, all or none of your toes touching the mattress? Is the side of one of your feet lying on the sheet but the heel isn't? Which part of your other foot is on the mattress? It takes effort to pinpoint each piece of your body and how it feels in relation to the mattress, and your mind may drift back to your thoughts. When you notice this happening, return to the last body part you remember and continue with the scan.

This isn't something to rush. The desired outcome isn't that you get to the top of your head but that you become so bored or tired of this exercise that you fall asleep. If you feel uncomfortable and want to shift position, do so. You can restart the body scan exercise as many times as you need to. If you reach the top of your head you can move position and start again, perhaps scanning in the opposite direction from your head to your feet.

Every time your mind wanders off to worrying, go through the same process: acknowledge your thoughts, give yourself compassion for how difficult this feels, and bring your focus back to where your body is in contact with the mattress.

And if you still can't sleep?

Try to keep your thoughts as positive as you can. Think of three things that have brought you happiness or comfort. Continue to focus not on the sleep you're not getting, but on the sensation of your body within the bed as it touches the mattress and duvet, and the rise and fall of your breathing.

Sleep will come!

> 'There are those who give with joy,
> and that joy is their reward'
>
> Kahlil Gibran

Lend a hand

Whether it's helping out in a charity shop or painting a village hall, volunteering is a rewarding experience that individuals, groups and whole communities can benefit from

Although many people like the idea of volunteering, life can get in the way. When it already feels as though there aren't enough hours in the day, finding additional time to dedicate to others can be tough.

If it wasn't for committed volunteers, though, many charities, community groups and organisations would not be able to exist. They rely on people donating money, but equally depend on individuals giving their time and skills. Marshals are needed to guide runners safely around a marathon route; leaders are required to inspire young girls in a Brownie pack; listeners are vital to support the weary at the end of a helpline. Without volunteers many events wouldn't happen, clubs wouldn't survive and services wouldn't be available.

Taking that first step and putting yourself forward as a volunteer, whether on a regular or more ad hoc basis, can be the start of an incredibly rewarding journey. Within no time, you'll notice the joy you bring to others – and a new-found pleasure in your life too.

Where to start

There are a few questions you need to ask yourself before you take that first step

Who would you like to help?
There's a wealth of community groups, organisations and charities that run purely on the hard work of volunteers. Volunteers run libraries, day centres, youth groups, even film clubs, while there are cafes up and down the country that rely on the goodwill of others to serve tea and bake cakes. Charities also depend on volunteers to stand with collecting buckets at events or during fundraising weeks.

List ideas here

....

....

....

....

....

....

....

....

How much time can you commit?

Be realistic when considering the time you can dedicate. Volunteering needs to be something you look forward to, not another chore you dread. If you can't commit regularly, consider other options. Maybe you could take part in a beach clean-up in the summer or plant bulbs for a retirement home ready for spring.

Time you could spare

....

....

....

....

....

....

Do you want to use the skills you already have, or learn new ones?

Maybe you're an IT whizz, handy with a camera or you love to knit. Whether you use these skills at work or they're just hobbies, thinking about what you can do and what you'd like to do can be a great way of sparking ideas and opportunities.

Skills you have, and those you'd like to learn

....

....

....

....

....

....

Where to look

Once you have an idea of what you want to do, ask around locally – look in newspapers, enquire at the Women's Institute or the parish church. Or visit do-it.org.uk, a website that makes volunteering easy. Simply pop in your postcode and a list of local opportunities appear.

Mind how you grow

Tending a garden can bring you closer to nature than merely being outside, and the bond developed can help nourish body and soul

Most people instinctively know that time spent in the garden is beneficial – physically, mentally and spiritually. That's because, at its most enriching, gardening is a more reflective activity than simply doing or having.

This is where the concept of mindful gardening is so helpful. Being mindful is being present in the moment and holding that attention on an activity. When the mind drifts to dwelling on the past or worries about the future, it is brought back to the present. In her book, *RHS Gardening for Mindfulness*, Holly Farrell explains further: 'In mindful practice we need an anchor to bring our focus back every time our attention wanders. For sitting mindfulness practice this is the rise and fall of the breath, but in the garden we can use our senses as the anchor instead. Nature calls on all our senses in a garden, grounding us in the present moment, so that we are able not only to get off autopilot but also to free ourselves from the past and future worries.'

Growing your own vegetables

A great place to start with mindful gardening is growing your own vegetables. Imagine a summer's day when you plan a salad for dinner and you pick rocket, radish, peppers, tomatoes and spring onions straight from the garden. Fresh, nutritious, delicious and all easy to grow. What's more, you don't need heaps of space for a greenhouse, vegetable plot or raised beds. If only a small patio or courtyard sits outside your kitchen door, these veg will happily grow in pots, small sacks or a hanging basket. Some will even flourish on a sunny windowsill.

Before you can bask in the glory of having grown your own veg, you'll need to invest in a few basic items. A hand trowel is useful, and you'll need a selection of pots. Make sure there are drainage holes in the bottom and use pot feet or bricks to raise them off the ground otherwise the holes will get blocked.

Plastic pots are lighter and easier to clean than clay ones and will probably be cheaper. A bulkier purchase is compost. Multi-purpose compost should suffice for most vegetables. There may be a little trial and error at first, especially for beginners, but you'll be amazed by what you can achieve with very little effort. In no time at all, your confidence will grow alongside your vegetables.

Six easy veg to grow

Gardening is a waiting game and it can take time to see the best results. That said, when growing vegetables some crops will be ready to eat only a month after sowing and there's nothing better to motivate you to grow more.

Sowing seeds is relatively straightforward. Just pop them thinly on a layer of soil and cover with a little more compost. Remember that one packet of seeds often equates to dozens of plants. You'll usually find the number of seeds listed on the back. In some cases, it's easier to buy a young plant at a garden centre than to sow seeds early that then need space indoors to germinate. If you do find yourself with an excess of plants, speak to friends and neighbours. They may be happy to do a swap.

Radish
Sow radish seeds direct into a pot and you'll see results in as little as three weeks – it's the ultimate fast food. For the best peppery taste, pick radishes when still small and tender. Plants will tolerate a little shade but don't let them dry out. Radishes are rich in potassium and vitamin C.

Sow direct: March to September
Harvest crops: April to November

Garlic
Although it takes a while to grow, once you've tasted the intense flavour of garlic from the garden, you'll realise it was worth the wait. Buy either individual cloves or a whole head of garlic, which you then separate, from the garden centre. You'll need deep pots, or use a potato-growing sack, and bury the cloves, pointed end facing up, 2in (5cm) below the surface. Keep moist but don't over water. Shoots will pop up and then wither. At this point, your garlic is ready.

Sow direct: February to March, October to December
Harvest crops: June to August

Potatoes
Don't be too confused by the different 'first earlies', 'second earlies', 'early maincrop' terms. All you need to know is to plant earlies by early April and maincrops by the end of the month. Buy potato tubers from garden centres and allow them to chit – put in an empty egg box in a cool, dark place. When you see a few new nodules, plant three tubers in around 4in (10cm) of multi-purpose compost at the bottom of a deep growing sack. As they grow and new shoots appear, cover with more compost. Do this two or three times until the sack is almost full. When the shoots flower, have a feel around to see if the potatoes are big enough to lift.

Sow direct: February to April
Harvest crops: May to October

Rocket

Rocket grows quickly. You'll be able to harvest your first crop and enjoy spicy leaves within four to six weeks of sowing. Sow seeds thinly straight into a pot or, if you eat a lot of salad, sow a growbag of mixed salad leaves. Pick leaves frequently with your hand or scissors to encourage further growth.

Sow direct: March to September
Harvest crops: April to November

Tomatoes

Okay, so tomatoes are technically a fruit, but they are still very easy to grow, especially the bushy Tumbler variety that is perfect for hanging baskets. Grown outdoors in full sun, they'll be packed with vitamin C. Fill the basket, or pot if you prefer, with growbag compost, then pop in the young plant. Don't allow the soil to dry out – you may need to water twice a day in the height of summer. Again, hand-pollinate the flowers and, once you see fruit, regularly feed with tomato plant food.

Buy young plants: April to June
Harvest crops: June to October

Courgettes

You'll only need one or two courgette plants (each can produce up to 30 fruit), so it's easier to buy young plants. A large pot around 2ft (60cm) in diameter is required but, once planted, the courgette can be left to go about its own business. Keep plants well watered and regularly check for slugs, who love courgettes. Courgettes are a good source of vitamins A, C and E, and the yellow flower is also edible.

Buy young plants: May to July
Harvest crops: July to October

Garden notes

Record the evolution of your plants and jot down any tips and ideas for next year

....

....

....

....

....

....

....

....

....

....

....

....

....

....

....

....

....

....

....

....

....

....

....

Detox

Forget the hype about specific detox plans and drinks. You can make your own personalised plan with just a few changes

Everyone has times throughout the year when they overindulge, eating and drinking to excess. Although at the time it may feel good and the right thing to do, it can also leave you feeling sluggish. Afterwards, many people begin to think about getting healthy again, and that's where the word 'detox' may come up.

Do you really need to detox your body?

You may remember from biology lessons at school that your body is constantly detoxing, filtering out waste products from bodily functions, removing toxins such as alcohol and chemicals from pollution. Several organs are involved: skin, intestines, liver and kidneys. Pills, patches, potions and lotions cannot do these intricate processes for you, which is why keeping your body in tip-top shape is essential for staying fit and well.

What about special diets?

Typical detox diets (also known as fad diets) often promote an extreme restriction of calories and eliminate food groups. This is not only unnecessary, but is likely to result in weight loss followed by regain, and, even worse, a return to old, poorer eating patterns. Going on a restrictive eating plan doesn't tend to promote healthy habits, and if you restrict calories too much then you may not have the energy needed to perform daily activities in addition to exercise. In the long term, starting a plan usually leads to finishing a plan, and then what? You can, however, put in place a few changes to revamp your diet after a period of indulgence.

Will it help psychologically?

Although your body naturally detoxes on a daily basis, there is something to be said for doing it to help your psychological wellbeing. Some people like to have a defined period of time where they follow a specified healthy eating plan to kickstart their new healthier regime. Others may feel that following a restricted eating plan leaves them craving the foods that they have omitted. However you feel, taking time out to relax and getting to bed at a decent time is bound to make you feel a whole lot better. It will also leave you more in control of your (healthy) choices the next day.

What should I eat in a day?

Here is an example of a healthy diet, perfect after a period of overindulging. These meals are rich with nutrients to satisfy your body and the combination of protein, low GI carbs and healthy fats will keep you feeling fuller for longer.

Breakfast Smashed avocado with poached eggs and cherry tomatoes on rye bread

Mid-morning snack One apple with 1–2tbsp nut or seed butter

Lunch A large bowl of vegetable and lentil or bean soup

Mid-afternoon snack A small piece of cheese and a handful of grapes

Evening meal Baked salmon with sweet potato wedges, tenderstem broccoli and asparagus

Dessert or supper Greek yoghurt with blueberries, honey and cinnamon

Drinks 1–3 cups of green or black tea, water or warm water with lemon (which is caffeine-free)

Eat more superfoods

Eating more salads is another great way to incorporate a wide range of fresh fruit and vegetables (aka wholesome superfoods) into your diet. The advice is to eat at least five 3oz (80g) portions of fruit, vegetables or salad a day. There is also evidence to suggest that people who regularly eat salads with a meal actually eat fewer calories overall, while still feeling satisfied.

Nutrients vary by the type of salad leaf (which make the perfect base of a salad), but the very popular lettuce can be a source of vitamin A, folate and manganese, and a good source of vitamin K.

Salads are not only healthy and quick to prepare, they are also versatile and convenient. Add olive oil, avocado and nuts to help aid nutrient absorption.

Make your perfect superfood salad

- **Choose your salad base** – for example, watercress, baby leaf salad, spinach, lambs' lettuce, iceberg, herb salad, rocket or pea shoots.

- **Add protein** – try grilled chicken breast, boiled egg, tuna (canned in water), salmon or feta cheese. Protein contains amino acids, which contribute to the growth and maintenance of lean muscle mass.

- **Add a rainbow of vegetables** – including cherry tomatoes, cucumber, beetroot, radishes, celery, pepper or red onion. People should eat a 'rainbow' of foods to ensure that they are consuming a wide variety of different nutrients.

- **Add a slow-release starchy carbohydrate** – such as brown basmati rice, quinoa, wholemeal pitta bread, sweet potato, granary bread or wholemeal pasta. Carbohydrate supplies our body with the energy needed for the maintenance of normal brain function and fibre.

- **Add a light, tasty dressing** – such as olive oil and lemon juice. If you're making your own, add the oil and vinegar in a 3:1 ratio along with any other ingredients – try black pepper, maple syrup, pesto, balsamic vinegar, sweet chilli sauce (but check the main ingredient isn't sugar), light mayonnaise or a light French dressing.

- **And finally, jazz it up with toppings** – olives, avocado, flaked almonds, apple pieces, raisins, cashews, pine nuts, toasted walnuts, anchovies or pomegranate seeds are all great-tasting options.

Diet makeover

- Ditch (or decrease) your intake of sweets, chocolate, cakes, biscuits, crisps and fizzy drinks (i.e. added sugars).

- Eat an abundance of whole foods including fruit, vegetables, fish, nuts, seeds, lean meat and whole grains.

- Top up with water (fluid) regularly throughout the day to stay hydrated and alert.

- Open up to relaxing, taking more me-time and sleeping (aim for seven to eight hours a night).

- Exercise (or move your body daily) – aim for 30 minutes of moderately intense activity at least five times a week, including two sessions of resistance exercise.

What about your environment?

The first thing you should do when embarking on a healthy living mission is to make your environment conducive to weight loss and healthy eating. Go straight to the kitchen and detox it. Don't rely on willpower. It's like a muscle: the more it's used throughout the day, the weaker it gets. This means that you may be most vulnerable to tempting offers of high fat or sugar foods in the evening.

Take the pressure off yourself by getting rid of any chocolates (you could give them away) and stock up with lots of fresh fruit and vegetables. Cook in bulk so that a healthy meal is never too far away. Organise your fridge so that you have healthy snacks such as pre-cut veggies and hummus or salsa, boiled eggs and cherry tomatoes or chicken slices at eye level. Keep higher calorie foods on lower shelves and cover them in tin foil (so that your eyes aren't drawn to them).

Keep a food diary

A food diary can be a useful place to start. This will help to increase mindfulness of foods eaten and may give you an insight into anything you're overlooking – is missing lunch causing you to dig into that packet of crisps? If so, make your lunch in advance and put temptations out of sight.

Record everything you eat and drink over the course of a week

MONDAY

Breakfast

....

....

....

....

....

Lunch

....

....

....

....

Dinner

....

....

....

....

Snacks

....

....

....

....

....

TUESDAY

Breakfast

....
....
....
....
....
....

Lunch

....
....
....
....
....

Dinner

....
....
....
....
....

Snacks

....
....
....
....
....

WEDNESDAY

Breakfast

....

....

....

....

....

Lunch

....

....

....

....

....

Dinner

....

....

....

....

....

Snacks

....

....

....

....

....

....

THURSDAY

Breakfast

....
....
....
....
....
....

Lunch

....
....
....
....
....

Dinner

....
....
....
....
....

Snacks

....
....
....
....
....
....

FRIDAY

Breakfast

....
....
....
....
....
....

Lunch

....
....
....
....

Dinner

....
....
....
....

Snacks

....
....
....
....
....

SATURDAY

Breakfast

....
....
....
....
....
....

Lunch

....
....
....
....
....

Dinner

....
....
....
....
....

Snacks

....
....
....
....
....

SUNDAY

Breakfast

....
....
....
....
....

Lunch

....
....
....
....

Dinner

....
....
....
....

Snacks

....
....
....
....
....

An open look at problems

It's tempting to ignore disputes, issues and worries in the hope they'll go away, but facing problems head on and taking a considered, logical approach can help you to move forward

They have a habit of appearing out of the blue in off-guard moments. They can be physical, psychological or a combination of the two and range in seriousness, type and size. Some are manageable or easily solved while others can remain hidden only to resurface unexpectedly. A few can throw your life into turmoil, cause years of suffering and even threaten your very existence. Such is the power of problems.

Many, of course, such as financial concerns, short-term medical conditions or mechanical hiccups, are part and parcel of routine life and have well-established solutions and interventions. Others can be trickier or more personal and require more than a trip to the bank, a spell in A&E or the purchase of a new wing mirror for a car. These unexpected problems can leave you bewildered, test your resilience and in some cases undermine your internal world.

A measured response

How problems are perceived and responded to will differ from person to person, and reactions can be influenced by several factors and vary from day to day. Instinctive, gut responses are common and usually take place immediately or soon after an initial period of shock or disbelief. The emotional outpourings vary widely and include frustration, anxiety, helplessness, remorse and anger. In some cases this can lead to verbal and physical retaliation, bullying on social media platforms and even self-harm. In others, the response can cause more suffering than the initial problem itself. It's easy to overreact in the heat of the moment only to regret it later or to dwell for days on the killer line that would have won an argument.

But non-emergency problems can be approached in a more considered way, one where the brain, logic and inner human nature take charge. This involves a conscious reaction as opposed to one that originates from the gut. One such approach is consciously to meet it (face it), greet it (consider the options) and beat it (employ solutions). This can maximise your chance of reaching a satisfactory resolution.

1 Meet it

This involves looking at problems head on before analyzing and dealing with them in a conscious way. If there is something that bothers you to the extent that it causes behaviours or emotions you regard as negative, then make a concerted effort to resolve the issue rather than turning a blind eye to it and letting it fester. Dealing with problems can make you stronger.

If there is a truly insurmountable problem, the only choice may be to accept it fully to move forward in life, so it stops unnecessary or prolonged suffering. This doesn't mean you have given in, just that you have been mature enough to put it to bed for good. The time such acceptance takes will vary. Sometimes a physical ritual can help – burning a candle, for instance, and agreeing with yourself that when the candle dissolves or goes out, so does the problem.

The mind, however, can ignore instructions and continue to churn issues over and over. If a problem you have agreed to accept resurfaces in your head, be disciplined and remind yourself that it is not a dilemma any longer. Your mind should learn to listen to your conscious effort and approach.

2 Greet it

It might help to think about a problem logically to assess its nature, size and scale because the mind can make matters appear worse than they are. Sometimes the availability of a solution might dictate how bad a problem is. Have you ever stressed about something only to find the answer was simple and easily available?

Ask yourself the following questions and try to challenge your understanding of the issue. Recording your thoughts can help to organise them.

Is there a real dilemma to be solved or is your perception of an issue making it appear like a problem?

....

....

....

....

....

....

....

....

....

Can someone truly upset you or is your reaction something learned, a response mechanism that you might be able to control or change?

....

....

....

....

....

....

....

....

....

....

....

If you are responsible for the way you respond, can you choose to respond differently in future, especially with similar problems?

....

....

....

....

....

....

....

....

....

....

....

Often, past events continue to draw focus and be experienced as problems. It might be worth asking if they are still a concern now or whether it is the mind churning them up. Should you be suffering because of something that happened in the past and is categorically in the past? Is it possible to solve these problems?

There are several questions that can be asked to ensure appropriate solutions can be identified and your response is fair, measured and reasonable.

Do you need help from others?

Whose responsibility is it (if anyone's) to deal with the problem?

Does it automatically fall to you?

Are you accepting too much responsibility?

Could the solution be a joined-up effort with others?

Is speaking up the right thing to do, even if it may not go down well?

Some people tend to keep problems to themselves as they are mindful of the impact on loved ones, but there are times when talking to family or friends can help. If that isn't possible, discussing an issue with a person who doesn't know you, such as a counsellor, network group or volunteer on a charity helpline, can be useful. Some firms also offer employee assistance programmes.

Consciously evaluating the size and scale of a problem, as well as your perception and response to it, can help to identify appropriate solutions. Having thought it through, your response is more likely to be measured and logical and stand a better chance of reaching a satisfactory resolution.

List the solutions available to you here, then perhaps seek advice on them from trusted friends or discreet colleagues

....

....

....

....

....

....

....

....

....

3 Beat it

Now you have to employ the solution. This may be a change of perception, full acceptance or another targeted but conscious effort. It may be a phased approach and require a series of planned steps involving honest and difficult conversations. But having done the mental preparation, your rationale will be clear in your own mind and make the prospect of an advantageous outcome more likely.

If the nature of the problem means it might re-emerge or fluctuate over time, it is worth noting your thought processes and actions here so that you can re-examine what went well, what could be improved and what might be best avoided. It will also help you to see if any proposed solutions are still appropriate.

This isn't intended to be a checklist. Its main purpose is to encourage a conscious and considered response to issues that arise rather than one that is triggered by gut reaction. This may help you to find effective solutions to life's problems and in turn improve your wellbeing. A tricky problem requires careful thought – meet it, greet it and beat it.

Your thoughts and actions

....

....

....

....

....

....

....

....

....

....

....

....

....

....

....

....

Remains of the day

Evenings have a distinctive mood. Whether it's the fading light at sunset or that satisfying sensation of knowing you have a few quality hours to do whatever brings you joy, there's a gentle energy that speaks to the soul and welcomes comforting rituals

Unwinding after a busy day is essential for your wellbeing, and contributes to a restful night's sleep. But the evening is also a magical time to be inspired and appreciative of life. When you're mindful about how you spend the evening hours, you can ensure a fulfilling close to the day.

Although evenings offer an opportunity to rest, reflect and restore balance, what you actually do with these hours depends on your own energetic rhythms and needs. Some people prefer being alone to enjoy a cosy night in with a good book or a creative project, while others opt for a livelier end to the day and enjoy dancing or dining with family and friends. Some people prefer to stick to the same evening routine day in, day out, while others like spontaneity and variety so that no two evenings are identical. How you wish to spend your evenings is really up to you... as long as you believe you're spending your time well.

If, however, your evenings seem to disappear into a blur of tiredness, or leave you feeling dull, bored or empty, then it could be time to consider how you can make this time more fulfilling.

Do whatever lights you up. Establish what you need. If your days are hectic and full of chatter, you might relish tranquil, quiet evenings. If you work alone, then you may prefer your evenings to be sociable and fun. Perhaps you need an evening routine that will aid a restful night's sleep and a more organised start to the next day. Maybe you're keen to write in your journal or focus on a creative project. Once you know your priorities, you can make the most of these hours before darkness.

Remember, though, there is no 'one evening fits all'. What you do towards day's end is a personal choice and depends upon your circumstances. What's important is that you choose to spend your evenings in a way that nurtures and enriches you. Those precious hours before sleep are an opportunity to appreciate life, to plan and create, or simply to relax, and you'll wake the next morning feeling happier, revitalised and primed for your day.

How to make the most of your evenings

Plan
Decide how you want to spend your evening and then make space for that to happen. This might mean making minor changes to existing commitments with your partner, family or friends. Establish what time you have available and what you need to put in place to enjoy these few hours.

Unplug
Technology is a wonderful thing, but a constant preoccupation with the internet, social media, screen-scrolling, television channel hopping and gaming consumes time and disconnects you from yourself and your loved ones. During the evening, unplug or limit your use of your computer, phone and other electronics. It's better for wellbeing and evidence suggests it can lead to a more restful night's sleep.

Exercise
Ease the day out of your mind and muscles with gentle exercise. Try yoga, tai chi, a short cycle ride or a stroll in the park.

Meditate
A brief early-evening meditation can clear the day's noise and let you step into the later hours feeling calm and refreshed.

Embellish
It's the little things that often make the difference. Embellish your cosy evening space by lighting scented candles, playing soothing music or snuggling up in your favourite blanket.

Create
Evenings offer a wonderful time to get creative. Start that writing or art project you've always wanted to do. Learn to sew or knit. Take up pottery. Experiment!

Read
There is nothing quite like spending an evening engrossed in a good story. Reading will help you detach from the day and is one of the most popular pre-sleep rituals.

Stargaze
On a clear night, find a few moments to look at the stars before you go to bed. It's deeply calming and will put your day and any troubles into perspective.

Sleep
A refreshing night's sleep is the goal at the end of a well-spent evening. Establish a good routine. Know exactly how many hours you need to be at your best and what you have to do to ensure you'll be well rested and revitalised when you wake.

Write
Put pen to paper and write down your thoughts, feelings and ideas in this journal. This evening ritual lets you release the mind's chatter so you can look forward to a restful sleep.

ORGANISE

Do all the small chores that will bring you peace of mind and prepare you for the next day. Spend part of your evening tidying up, preparing food and generally getting ready to start a new day with freshness and purpose.

Your to-do list

....

....

....

....

....

....

....

....

....

....

REFLECT

Founding father of the USA, Benjamin Franklin, had a dedicated daily schedule and a specific evening review. Every night he asked himself: 'What good have I done today?' This evening ritual only took a few minutes, but provided honest reflection and encouraged him to achieve more good in his life.

How has your day been?

....

....

....

How do you feel? Celebrate your joy and achievements

....

....

....

....

APPRECIATE

Take a few moments to appreciate what's in your life. Write about it here or add a note to your gratitude jar. Appreciating and expressing gratitude for all that is positive and loving in your life is a good way to close the evening.

People who make you smile

....
....
....
....
....
....
....
....
....
....
....
....

The wonder of nature

....
....
....
....

Think of an act of kindness – no matter how small – that touched your soul

....
....
....
....

You
can
do it

Why bother?

People are often their own worst critics. But this tendency to judge yourself harshly can prevent you from enjoying life to the full. Switch on your I CAN mode to rekindle a sense of joy and optimism

Do you too often feel disheartened? Feelings of gloom can descend without warning, depending on what's going on in your life: from feeling like you're putting more into a relationship than you're getting out of it, to being undervalued at work. Sometimes things just seem to be conspiring against you. And it's at times like these it can be easy to think to yourself: 'Why bother?'

It doesn't have to be this way. The quicker you are able to break the cycle of these habitual negative emotions, the quicker you will be able to reconnect and rekindle your more natural sense of optimism, hope and fun.

Let's start by putting things into perspective. People have at least 40,000 thoughts per day and an estimated 70 per cent of those are negative. The brain is inclined towards a negativity bias. What does this mean?

Like all mammals, humans are wired up to be prepared for the worst in order to secure their basic survival. However, in the modern world, when worries are more likely to refer to money, jobs or families (and not the imminent threat of an animal attack), this negative bias can become a destructive habit, rather than a life-saving one. The flipside is that everyone is capable of wonder, uplifting emotions and extraordinary states of mind that feed curiosity and cultivate a sense of meaning.

How do you flip that switch in your head when you're stuck in a negative groove?

....

....

....

....

....

....

....

Switch on your 'I CAN' mode

Being in a negative state of mind can sap you of energy and motivation. It puts you on a downward spiral that grinds your life to a halt.

The antidote is vitality and you can start tapping into that energy by using your imagination – your very own reality generator.

If you can internally connect with your own personal talents, resources and qualities (not things necessarily valued by others but those which give you meaning), you'll instantly feel more of an 'I CAN' attitude to life.

To do this, first take time to remind yourself of your strengths and qualities; let the feelings that arise permeate through your consciousness. Perhaps you feel that you're a kind person, that you're courageous, maybe you value your wit or generosity – focus on these strengths. Record them here and try to get into the habit of reading them daily. It may feel strange at first, but soon they will begin to sink in and you will start to believe in them.

Your strengths and qualities

....

....

....

....

....

....

....

....

....

....

....

....

....

....

You CAN do it

Next, think of an activity, role or relationship that brings you meaning and happiness. This could be as simple as reminding yourself of something you used to do, such as playing an instrument, participating in team sports or painting landscapes. Remember and re-live times when you were able to show your best self and feel how this ignites motivation in you. Motivation is the natural bridge to action; to stepping out and living your life more fully.

Times you've felt happy

....
....
....
....
....
....
....
....
....
....
....
....
....
....
....
....
....
....
....

Do
what
you
Love

What does joy mean to you? Don't think too much.
Just list all the words and feelings that come to mind

Meet your inner coach

If you dig a little deeper, beyond your immediate worries, you'll uncover one of the greatest and most hidden causes of your gloom and fatigue: your inner critic. That constant nagging voice that wears everyone down. That voice that indignantly says you're not beautiful enough, not clever enough and you have ideas above your station. 'Who do you think you are?' it demands.

Learn to break that negative default setting by uncovering your inner coach or friend. It could be the voice of someone who has encouraged you in the past, or perhaps you can find the voice of your own kindness and generosity that you offer to other people.

When the negative inner critic tries to take hold, call upon your inner friend or coach. Ask yourself: 'What would my encouraging inner mentor say now?' and 'How would she make me feel?'

Record your thoughts here

....
....
....
....
....
....
....
....
....
....
....
....

All it takes is 10 to 15 seconds and you will notice an internal change. You'll find cracks appearing in that negative armour, allowing the light of positive thinking to infiltrate and improve your mood.

Cultivating an 'I CAN' approach to life and learning to listen to your inner coach, rather than giving in to the fears of your inner critic, will lead you towards a more upbeat and energetic life, full of vitality.

Comfort and joy

Cultivating positive habits and practices is key to helping you reconnect with the pleasure of living. Here are some ideas to set you on your way:

1 Take daily walks
British author Virginia Woolf would walk round London every day. Mingling with people and being curious would give her new ideas and refresh her thinking.

2 Make time for solitude
Get better acquainted with yourself and the different voices within – coach as well as critic – by finding a way to disconnect every day.

3 Seek out your friends
Connect with people from the past who don't cross your path every day. Send them an email, give them a call for no other reason than to tell them you're thinking of them and want to know how they are. These small gestures generate a huge amount of pleasure and inspiration.

4 Make an 'artist's date'
In her bestselling classic *The Artist's Way*, author Julia Cameron recommends booking a weekly 'artist's date' – time set aside to go on an excursion for at least two hours. Do anything out of the ordinary: go to a paint shop, walk along the beach, collect leaves on a walk, attend a concert. This activity will help realign your perspective and ignite your creativity.

5 Talk to strangers
Be curious about, and listen to, people you don't know. Find opportunities to strike up exchanges and conversations with strangers. Social interactions can be predictable. Strangers invariably make you see the world in a different way.

6 Get stuck in and use your hands
Touch directly affects the autonomic nervous system and calms you down. Instantly transport yourself through pottery, cooking, gardening, sewing, drawing or playing an instrument.

Ways you could reconnect with your optimistic side

One word

Choosing a single word to guide you through life's challenges can have a surprisingly big impact

The practice of choosing a word and allowing it to guide you is nothing new. In January 2006, Ali Edwards, a designer, author and workshop instructor who blogs at aliedwards.com, selected a word to focus on for 12 months while going about her daily life. The word she chose was 'play'. 'I thought a lot about play and what it means to me,' she writes. 'For me, it was a lot about living without fear – about being more open to experiences with an attitude of playfulness.' The exercise was so successful that Ali has spent the years since repeating it with different words. Among others they have included 'peace', 'nurture', 'vitality', 'open' and 'thrive'.

Part of Ali's tradition involves asking readers to send in their words, which she compiles into a master list – these make for fascinating reading. Who would have guessed, for example, that 'aroha' (the Maori word for love and affection) would ever appear, or that 'geek' could be an inspirational term? Most of the words, however, fall into one of two categories. They either describe things people would like to add to their lives, or things they would like to remove. The word 'peace', for example, makes a regular appearance, while the word 'fearless' is a popular choice. In 2011, Ali's friend, Liz Lamoreux, read out that year's list and sent the audio file to Ali. The result is a poem of sorts – hopes, fears, intentions and emotions laid bare. The contributors are united by their resolve to instigate change in their lives. Liz now reads the new list every year.

Word of choice

So how do you choose a word? And what do you do with it? Well, sometimes the best course of action is to let a word choose you. Is there something you keep saying, or thinking, to yourself? Maybe you look around your house and feel overwhelmed by the amount of stuff you own. If so, why not pick a word that encourages you to take positive action – 'declutter', 'simplify' or 'purge', for example? Better still, choose a word that sums up how you would like to feel once your house is clutter free: 'calm', 'peaceful' or 'relaxed', for example. The most important thing is to choose a word that speaks to you, and try not to be swayed by other people's opinions. The word you choose needs to make you feel excited, empowered and energised. You need to be in love with this word!

Put it on display

Once you have settled on a word, make sure that it is somewhere that is visible to you every day. You could write it on a piece of paper and slip it into your diary or journal. But don't use any old scrap of paper – this is an important word. Instead, find a beautifully designed card or a vintage notelet and write your word with confidence and a flourish. You could even have your word engraved on a piece of jewellery, or cut out of wood or acrylic and hung on a wall. The way you display your word is entirely up to you, however it does need to be visible, to act as a prompt.

Maybe buy a box of beautifully designed alphabet cards, or make your own. Every so often, take down the cards and use them to spell out a word. Pick a prominent shelf or windowsill to display them on, and clear away any surrounding clutter. You want the word to have space to breathe and take on an air of importance in the room. Once in position, the word will become your guiding light for the coming days and weeks. Read your word aloud every day. Turn it into a mantra.

Keep it fresh

It's okay to change your word if you no longer find it helpful – don't be a slave to it. The word you have chosen might only be relevant to a specific project or certain period in your life. If so, let it go. But make a note of it all the same, because looking through lists of previous word choices can tell you a great deal about who you are and who you hope to become.

You can let your word percolate, subtly influencing your actions, or you can use it more directly to assist you in decision-making. If you get a bit lost, stop what you're doing and ask yourself what you can do right now to honour your word. If you have chosen 'declutter', for instance, why not throw away all the old, dried-up pens on your desk? Similarly, if your word is 'calm', take a couple of mindful breaths, no matter where you are or what you are doing. They may be small steps, but each one will carry you closer to your goal.

Take the word 'respond', for instance. This might remind you that while you may not be able to change certain events in your life, you can choose the way you respond to them. It could be used to help you when you encounter challenges at work, or to calm you down when you feel impatient with a loved one or friend.

Focusing on one word can be powerful and lead to genuine life change. It can provide focus and comfort, and it can be liberating. It can teach you what you need most in your life, and go some way to suggest how you might achieve it. It's just one little word, but it can have a huge impact.

Your words

➤ ....
....

➤ ....
....

➤ ....
....

➤ ....
....

➤ ....
....

➤ ....
....

➤ ....
....

➤ ....
....

➤ ....
....

➤ ....
....

➤ ....
....

➤ ....
....

➤ ....
....

➤ ....
....

Crafting a better state of mind

Studies show that crafting reduces stress and anxiety,
and boosts positivity and connectedness

Creative activities are increasingly being recognised as a way of coping with problems such as anxiety and depression. Colouring as therapy, creative papercrafts, scrapbooking and peaceful needlecrafts such as knitting, crochet, embroidery and hand quilting can all be practised in conjunction with mindfulness techniques to produce a more spiritual experience – but even as standalone activities their benefits are clear.

In a quick-fix, disposable, consumer society, handmade gifts – for yourself or others – show care and attention. Then there's the crafting itself. It gives you something to do with your hands, it's a pleasingly tactile activity, and when you finish a project you have achieved something you can really be proud of.

Knitting is the new yoga

Knitting has been found to have benefits for health and wellbeing, and has even been called the new yoga. Former physiotherapist and knitter Betsan Corkhill has spent more than a decade looking into the way therapeutic knitting can make lives better. In her book *Knit for Health & Wellness*, she notes the way the rhythm of knitting can bring on a meditative state, calming knitters and helping them to think more clearly. The position of their hands can help them to feel their personal space is protected, while research has shown that the way the hands cross the midline of the body may affect the perception of pain.

Betsan writes: 'Studies in animals have shown that repetitive movement enhances the release of serotonin. Serotonin raises mood, but it also calms and is an analgesic. People often instinctively engage in repetitive, rhythmic movement when they are stressed or traumatised. They are intuitively self-soothing as they rock, pace or tap. Frequent knitting (more than three times a week) can help people feel calmer and happier, even those suffering from clinical depression.'

Other studies support Betsan's research. In a survey of more than 3,000 members of an online knitting community, 82 per cent said they felt happy after knitting, nearly half said it helped them think through their problems and nearly two-thirds reported an increase in confidence, according to research by the University of Exeter Medical School and De Agostini Publishing.

'You can't use up creativity. The more you use, the more you have.'

Maya Angelou

It sounds good on paper

One of the more surprising creative pastimes that has been linked to wellbeing is adult colouring books, the sales of which have taken off as more people look for a simple, tried and tested way to switch off from the stresses and strains of everyday life.

The craze may be relatively new, but psychologists and therapists have known about the benefits of colouring for a long time. Carl Jung, the Swiss psychiatrist who worked with Sigmund Freud and founded analytical psychology, recommended colouring to his patients, believing it would help them access their subconscious and self-knowledge. Today, psychologists encourage their patients to colour as a way to relax and meditate. This simple, easy activity – which for many will bring back memories of happier childhood days – can distract you from niggling problems and even help you to sleep. And it's been found to help with more serious problems too.

Those suffering from anxiety, stress and even post-traumatic stress disorder can find relief in colouring, which calms down the amygdala, the part of the brain responsible for the fight-or-flight response. On top of that, colouring can help with concentration, focus and fine motor skills, and is a great way of practising mindfulness. Counsellor Dr Nikki Martinez writes in the *Huffington Post*: 'There are many times when I suggest adult colouring books to my patients, and they look at me as though we should be switching seats. However, time and again, they come back to me and tell me how beneficial they find them.'

Therapists have also found that origami, the Japanese art of paper folding, helps with focus and concentration, and, because it requires patience, can help people to work through anger and frustration. Other paper crafts are just as beneficial. Countless studies have found that altruism and giving can help people connect socially and provide a buffer against stress. So, card-making and creating paper gifts will help you just as much as they help the person you're making them for, while combining the catharsis of journaling with beautiful paper crafts will leave you with a beautiful memory as well as a sense of release. So what are you waiting for? It's time to get crafting.

'The desire to create is one of the deepest yearnings of the human soul'
Dieter F. Uchtdorf

Five steps to mindful crafting

1 **Clear your workspace**
A clear space will help you find a clear state of mind and allow you to concentrate fully on your craft.

2 **Enjoy its tactile nature**
Focus on the different textures and sensations, and fully embrace the experience.

3 **Get into a rhythm**
Whether you're sewing, knitting, crocheting, embroidering, colouring, cutting or sticking, fall into a regular pace that suits you and enjoy the pattern.

4 **Feel the flow**
Getting really stuck into your craft can help you move into a meditative state, sometimes known as flow, which can ease symptoms of depression and anxiety.

5 **Be proud**
Whether you're working on a big project that will take months to finish, or a quick fix that leaves you with a beautifully finished object at the end of your session, take time to look at your work, enjoy it and acknowledge what you have accomplished.

Use the following colouring patterns to clear your mind and lighten your mood

Smarter connection

Establishing boundaries and being mindful of your online usage (as well as your reactions) means you're more likely to enjoy a beneficial relationship with social media

There are many positives to be found in the creation and growth of social media. Communication has broadened and reached further around the world because of it. It's done wonderful things to bring together like-minded people and to shrink the world virtually. People, who in previous decades would most likely never have met in real life, can find each other through similar interests, share their knowledge and in some cases create deep friendships and supportive communities.

But nothing is perfect, and there can be a downside. What people learn of a person through their status updates and posted photos doesn't represent their whole life. Social media posts are simply snapshots. Without a documentary crew following someone 24 hours a day, you have no way of knowing what their life is truly like. You don't know what struggles they wrestle with, what challenges they face, how they really feel or what they spend each waking moment doing. A photo on Instagram or a status post on Facebook only gives you a glimpse of a person and, as such, you can't accurately form an opinion of them or their life. That doesn't stop people trying, though.

What stories are you telling yourself?

How often do you scroll through social media, seeing images of a group of friends having fun or a beautifully decorated, tidy living room, and imagine the people who posted these photos live this way all the time? They're constantly having wonderful, carefree, fabulous experiences with their equally fabulous friends. Or their whole house is gorgeous, neat and perfectly styled, with no mess to be seen. There's a minuscule chance these stories are true: it's not impossible, but it is highly improbable. When you stop to think for a moment, you know that no one lives life as a 24/7 party. Everyone has to do the mundane, ordinary things at some point, usually every day, and no one spends every waking minute in a social whirlwind.

Just because people choose not to share the mess, but instead to post a moment that was happy, celebratory or particularly pretty, doesn't mean they're being inauthentic or presenting a fake version of themselves to the world. After all, who really wants to share photos of their family arguing, or the kitchen table covered in breakfast leftovers, random socks and unfinished homework? And who really wants to see them?

Social media posts are edited highlights of a person's life, they're not a documentary. Take these posts for what they are: snippets. Don't use them as an opportunity to make up stories about what someone's life is like or to compare it to your own. You can use status updates and photo posts as a positive prompt. Let someone's post about friends enjoying dinner together remind you to get in touch with a mate about meeting for a coffee or a glass of wine. Use photos you see of delicious-looking cakes as a reminder to try out that recipe you found, or to pop to the shops for a treat. If you scroll past an image of a stunning sunset, let it act as a reminder to look up from your phone and see the beauty in your patch of the world.

By being aware of how you're feeling, and what you're telling yourself as you scroll through social media, you're better able to see it for what it is, and not let it negatively impact your mood or feelings of self-worth. You can't control what others post, but you can decide how much of it you view and how you respond to it.

Notice how you feel before you start flicking through your favourite social media platforms, and think about how that changes as you scroll. If you start to feel fed up or dissatisfied, ask yourself why that is. What are you seeing that's changing your emotions?

....✿...

....

....

....

....

....

....

Challenge the assumptions you're making about the people behind the posts. Why do you think they have the perfect relationship/home/job/life? What's the concrete evidence that their life is wonderful? Even if it is, why should someone else's life diminish or elevate yours?

....

....

....

....

....

....

....

....

....

....

....

Your social media presence

As well as considering how you soak up and respond to social media, it's worth considering your personal contribution to the digital world. What you share is your choice and your responsibility. Once you've posted it online, it's out there, forever. You can limit who sees your updates to an extent, but it's still worth giving some thought to how posts could affect your life or that of your family.

A simple rule of thumb is that if you wouldn't say it in a room full of people, don't say it on social media. Think about who could see your posts – other family members, friends, colleagues, employers, customers? How will the people you feature in your posts feel about it, even in a few years' time?

Give some thought to how you're representing yourself to the outside world through your posts. Would people recognise it if they met you in the real world? Are the updates and messages you're putting out making a positive or negative contribution?

....

....

....

....

....

Keep a diary

Every time you see the number of likes on one of your posts or photos, you get little shots of dopamine and oxytocin that make you feel good and drive you to want more. This, in turn, makes you want to check your social media accounts more often, to see if anyone has liked or commented on your posts, and to experience those happy chemical hits again. You don't need to be a slave to social media addiction, however. It takes effort, but you can decide how much time you spend scrolling, and when to switch off.

Pay more attention to when and how often you flick through your social media and whether it's a good time to be doing it. Try keeping a social media diary – just for a day. Note down every time you check your accounts and for how long

....

....

....

....

Take a break

Before you move to tap once more on those little app icons, pause for a moment to consider why you're logging in.

Are you avoiding work? Are you looking for approval on your post?

....

....

....

....

What would happen if you didn't check in, and instead continued with what you were doing?

....

....

....

....

Challenge yourself to wait 10 more minutes before checking, set a timer if you need to. When the time is up and you flick through your social media accounts, was it worth the wait? Did you miss anything by waiting 10 minutes?

....

....

....

....

Establish your boundaries

Declaring a self-imposed digital ban for days on end is not necessarily practical or sustainable. But simple rules – say, no scrolling in the first hour of the day, while eating or after 9pm – may be more achievable.

Social media is a powerful and brilliant tool. But it is just that: a tool. You decide how often to use it, you choose how much of yourself to invest in it and you have a say in how you respond to other people's content. Use social media to connect with others, learn, find kindred spirits, be inspired, be motivated, share knowledge and see the beauty in the world.

Time to reflect

Use the changes in the seasonal cycle to tune into your natural intuition and consider what's going well for you – and what you need to focus on next

Most people have an innate compass that directs them towards what they need in their lives. Sometimes, though, it can be tricky to read its direction, and a period of reflection is needed. Often, there is no better time to do this than when the seasons change.

Life is not a straight path from beginning to end, but resembles cycles that vary and fluctuate. Most obvious is the 'diurnal' cycle, the 24-hour period around which most of the world operates, and which dictates men's hormonal patterns. Few question the benefits of sleeping at night and being active during the day.

Less commonly observed is the lunar cycle, which has measurable effects on behaviours and tendencies. People are more extroverted during the full moon and introverted during the new moon, for instance. Traditionally, Western culture honoured and cherished the seasonal cycle, but in recent years this has diminished in importance.

'The only way to make sense out of change is to plunge into it, move with it, and join the dance.'

Alan Watts

Yin and yang

With the seasons, there are times of rising and falling energy. In traditional Chinese medicine, these are characterised as yin and yang: yin for slow, dark, reflective, inward-looking; yang for fast, bright, energetic, outward-looking. Modern society promotes the idea of constantly being in a yang frame of mind.

People are supposed to be busy all the time, always socialising, getting things done, being active and looking out for others. But this goes against the wisdom of seasonal cycles. It is helpful to be active, productive and outgoing during the yang seasons (spring and summer), but it is also helpful to be quiet, still, reflective and introverted during the yin seasons (autumn and winter). This gives a long-lasting sense of balance, harmony and mental stability.

If you are sensitive to shifts in yin/yang energy, you may notice that your feelings are markedly different on the longest and shortest days of the year. For example, perhaps you are restless in the week or so before 21 June, the summer solstice in the Northern Hemisphere. The rising yang energy can be stimulating and many people are able to function quite effectively on less sleep.

Once the solstice has passed, there can be a sense of relief and relaxation. Although it is just the beginning of meteorological summer, the days are beginning to get shorter. This move back towards yin energy is welcome and refreshing.

During these periods, it's sensible to take extra care of health and wellbeing, and to listen to what your body wants you to do. Harmonising with nature and what is going on around you can be a great way to follow the natural rhythm of your body in connection with your surroundings.

As the time of the winter solstice in the Northern Hemisphere – 21 December – approaches, the season is one of reflection. It is strange that, on what is the most yin day of the year, many are shopping for gifts and going to parties when they might find an evening of quietness and withdrawal more beneficial.

You already know what you need

Intuition is one of the most powerful forms of bodily knowledge – most people know instinctively what they need in life. But it's easy to underestimate this.

Perhaps you are sceptical of intuition or have trouble identifying – or believing you have – intuitive feelings. If so, explore the following reflective activities and consider your responses. It could be you know the answers to some of the most pressing questions. You may even already know the direction you want your life to take, but so far you haven't trusted that small voice inside.

Take this opportunity to create an open space to listen to your answers, take them seriously and decide to take action on what you discover. It may turn out to be the start of a beautiful journey towards the places you most want to be.

Ready to reflect

Set aside time to try a few of these activities and, as you look back over your life, begin to tap into your intuition

Meditation moment

- If your mind is busy ruminating, all that mental chatter can block out your intuitive voice. Take a few moments to quieten your mind. Close the door, turn off your phone and move away from your computer.

- Take a few deep, slow breaths and feel your body start to relax. Focus your attention only on inhaling and exhaling. When thoughts come, picture them as clouds floating by in the sky. Then refocus on your breath.

- Now, keeping your eyes closed, cultivate a sense of reflection by thinking back over the past year. If a particular event pops up, stay with it for a while to see if the memory has any messages for you. Accept any thoughts or feelings as they come, acknowledge them and then let them go.

- This could take 10 minutes or half an hour – it's really up to you. After this process, you may find a renewed sense of direction and clarity.

Access your intuitive mind

Make a pendulum out of a coin or other small weight, sellotape and a length of string. When you hold this pendulum above a surface – say, a piece of paper – it will start swinging or moving depending on the imperceptible movements of your hand. The idea is that you can ask yourself simple questions that have a 'yes' or 'no' answer, and the pendulum will move a different way depending on what your intuitive answer to the question is. Perhaps your pendulum moves clockwise for 'yes' and anti-clockwise for 'no'. Or it could move in a circular fashion for 'yes' and a linear fashion for 'no'. Find out what your own pattern is by asking easy questions. Then ask yourself harder questions (with a 'yes' or 'no' answer) and see what your intuitive mind says. Eventually, over time, you won't need the pendulum in order to access your intuition. You will instantly know how you feel.

Question yourself

Write below a list of questions about what has happened to you over the past year. For example: *'What has made you happy? What have you appreciated?'* Focus on the positives as well as the negatives, and make sure to include space to think about problem areas as well as success stories. You could write: *'Has anything not happened that I wish had happened?'* or *'If I could change one thing about this year, it would be...'*. This task is not meant to be disheartening, simply eye-opening. If you feel you are getting stuck rehashing old events, shift your focus to more positive ones. The answers to these questions may not come to you immediately. Be prepared to sit with the questions and see what happens. Your answers, when they do come to mind, can be an excellent prompt for you to focus more on the things that truly make you happy going forward.

➤ ....
....
....

➤ ....
....
....

➤ ....
....
....

➤ ....
....
....

➤ ....
....
....

➤ ....
....
....

Free-writing

You can either free-write answers to the questions you listed previously or free-write anything that comes to mind. This is essentially a creative process where you put pen to paper and write whatever emerges in your head, without paying too much attention to the words or filtering or judging them. It can help to have a starting point. If you find yourself writing a list of events, perhaps try connecting to their emotional memories. Don't worry if what you have written does not make any sense. Free-writing works best when it is not structured or planned. Take some time away from what you have written and come back to it with a fresh mind. You may have a new view or begin to sense intuitive feelings about the direction in which you want to go.

....

....

....

....

....

....

....

....

....

....

....

....

....

....

....

....

....

....

Let's dance

Be it ballroom, ballet or bolero – or just good old bopping around the kitchen – the physical and psychological benefits of dancing are impressive. So, kick off your shoes and turn the music up – it's time to let your feet get happy

Just for kids?

The ability to escape to another world through the power of movement and music is a wonderful feeling. For many people, though, this natural inclination to dance – regardless of where they are or who they're with – becomes inhibited as the years pass, until finally it's reserved for family weddings or a surreptitious wiggle while stuck in traffic.

Why do people dance?

In prehistoric times dance was used as a form of communication, bonding and flirtation – a way to attract a mate. Current examples of the latter include the slow, seductive rumba, aka the 'dance of love', and the equally charged, but faster-paced Spanish flamenco, with its hand-clapping and foot-stomping. It can also symbolises a sense of belonging and identity: for example, the ceremonial village dances to mark the coming of age of a young Maasai warrior; or, the Morris dance, performed in England, which has its origins in the Cotswolds and celebrates the region's villages and people.

Why should people dance?

On a physical level, the cardiovascular element of simply moving your body more helps to strengthen the heart and lungs, which over time increases stamina. Bones become stronger, meaning reduced risk of osteoporosis. Muscles are also strengthened, and flexibility and posture improve. Add to that improved coordination and balance, and the all-over physical gains have the edge over many other activities.

Then there are the psychological benefits, which are equally impressive. Research by the Albert Einstein College of Medicine showed dance to have a significant impact on improving brain health, including a reduced risk of dementia as a result of the simultaneous combination of physical and cognitive demands. So, in a nutshell, the more you dance, the sharper you become.

Finally, comes the emotional upswing – or 'happy feet'. As Austrian writer Vicki Baum said: 'There are shortcuts to happiness and dancing is one of them.' But why? Firstly, mood-improving chemicals receive a huge boost, with the release of endorphins and increased production of serotonin and dopamine – the 'feel-good' hormones. Also, as you dance, your body and mind work in beautiful synergy and you become fully engaged in the music. This focus helps to reduce cortisol – the stress hormone – and promotes a sense of relaxation that helps people to manage stress levels more effectively. So, you're quite literally able to dance your cares away. It really doesn't matter whether you think you're any good at it. See it as playing and experimenting; laughing while learning.

Where do you start?

The popularity of television shows such as *Strictly Come Dancing* has fuelled an increase in demand for adult classes, and dance schools around the country are expanding their offerings to meet this demographic. In London, the Royal Academy of Dance (rad.org.uk) offers a range of beginner-level courses in ballet, contemporary and jazz aimed at adults with no previous experience, as well as the pioneering Dance for Lifelong Wellbeing project that provides the over-60s with free classes to improve their health and wellbeing.

There is also a plethora of village halls, leisure clubs and community centres offering the opportunity to sample anything from salsa to swing, as well as dance as meditation.

Do try this at home

Dancing with others not your thing? Then experience the wonderful freedom and enjoyment of dance at home. Try this exercise:

- **Choose your 'dance floor'.** Whether it's the kitchen, garage or bedroom, find a space where you feel relaxed and won't be disturbed.
- **Make yourself comfortable.** Wear clothes that will enable you to move freely. If possible, go barefoot. The soles of your feet are extremely sensitive; allowing them to make contact with the ground beneath you provides a comforting sense of grounding and connection.
- **Choose your soundtrack.** Maybe some old favourites that evoke happy memories, upbeat dance music to energise and uplift, or stirring classical tracks that transport you to beautiful landscapes. Choose something that really captures the way you want to feel.
- **Let it go.** Give yourself permission to really let go. Close your eyes, if that feels easier. Feel the music in your body and allow yourself to move with the rhythm. Whether a gentle sway, a steady shuffle, or wild arm-waving – do what feels good for you.
- **Notice the sensations.** What do you feel in your mind and body as you move? Connect with the emotions that are stirred. Allow your mind to let go of any negative thoughts. Allow any feelings of tension to be released from the body. Embrace the feeling of freedom and let it fill your heart. Invite those delicious ripples of euphoria to be absorbed from head to toe.
- **Relax, smile and, most importantly, enjoy.**

So, whether it's a carefully choreographed foxtrot, some creatively improvised contemporary, or a simple shimmy around the kitchen, it's proven that dancing is good for your health and wellbeing. It's time to set your inner child free and dance like there's no one watching.

'Dance is the hidden language of the soul, of the body'
Martha Graham

Fiction in a flash

How many words does it take to tell a story?
Welcome to the growing phenomenon of microfiction

'For sale: baby shoes, never worn.'

Legend has it that this was a novel in six words created by author Ernest Hemingway on the back of an envelope for a bet. The link to Hemingway may be spurious, but the tale answers a question that has intrigued writers and readers for decades: how many words do you need to tell a story?

Flash fiction is the generic term for very short fiction – generally defined as pieces between six and 1,000 words. The genre is gaining interest and importance, with a growing number of online magazines, competitions and anthologies dedicated to stories in varying degrees of brevity. 'It is definitely getting more popular,' says Joanna Sterling, who runs a website called The Casket of Fictional Delights, which combines her interest in collecting brooches with flash fiction. 'There are really quite mainstream competitions, and people see it as an entryway to getting into writing books because it's quite short to write.'

Flash fiction is also known as microfiction and has nearly as many names and sub-categories as words per story. Six words seems to be the minimum, a number picked not just for Hemingway's legendary 'novel', but also for a popular series of memoirs collected by US-based online storytelling magazine *Smith*. The publication's book, *Not Quite What I Was Planning: Six-Word Memoirs from Writers Famous & Obscure,* collected nearly 1,000 of these snippets, and became a *New York Times* bestseller that spawned follow-up collections on love and teenagers.

Twitterature

The next-shortest category is Twitterature: 140-character stories published on the social media site with the hashtag #TwitterFiction. *The Guardian* was so taken with the form that it asked 21 authors to come up with novels in 140 characters. Jeffrey Archer wrote: '"It's a miracle he survived," said the doctor. "It was God's will," said Mrs Schicklgruber. "What will you call him?" "Adolf," she replied.'

Helen Fielding's version was: 'OK. Should not have logged on to your email but suggest if going on marriedaffair.com don't use our children's names as password.' And S.J. Watson wrote: 'She thanks me for the drink, but says we're not suited. I'm a little "intense". So what? I followed her home. She hasn't seen anything yet.'

Nifty at fifty

The next step up is the 50-word dribble, followed by 55-word 55 Fiction, which itself is a sub-genre of the 100-word drabble, a format which has developed a huge following. The term was coined in Monty Python's *Big Red Book*, which described it as a word game where the first participant to write a novel was the winner. To make the game possible in the real world it was limited to 100 words, a concept believed to have originated in UK science-fiction fandom in the 1980s.

What makes a good piece of flash fiction?

Twists and turns. Kit de Waal, author of bestselling novel *My Name is Leon* and occasional judge of The Casket of Fictional Delights competition, is looking for 'a whole story that gives me depth and breadth, a beginning, a middle and an end but, just like a novel, not necessarily in that order! I'm looking for a turn in the story, something that propels it forward, maybe something unsettling or surprising. But I don't like gimmicks and tricks, I'm not keen on a rabbit out of the hat. For me, flash fiction has a sense of slow burn, something that will resonate with you long after the last word is read.'

Make every word count. Flash fiction writer and poet Meg Pokrass insists it's important to take your time over even the very shortest stories. She says: 'If one were writing a poem, would one think that because of the small word count, it could be dashed off? No. With poetry it is understood that revision is everything. It is the same way with flash.

'Editing and revising is the hard part, and most important. One must cut out every non-essential word with flash fiction, and work with use of language and imagery. Are the sentences beautiful? If not, you're going to lose the reader. Sometimes, a lengthy break is necessary – putting a story away and coming back to it much later. I often revise a piece for months and sometimes years before everything settles right.'

Reel the reader in. The Casket of Fictional Delights' Joanna adds: 'Even though a flash fiction doesn't have many words it still needs to tell a story, with a beginning, middle and end. Flash fiction is not poetry. It does not have to have swathes of descriptive detail or character development, but the reader must feel engaged and part of the narrative.'

Pen to paper

Use these tips to get your flash fiction off to a great start

Find your idea. 'I will get ideas from weird sources, like going to a news website and looking for the ones that are hidden,' says Erinna.

Search for inspiration. Website visualverse.org publishes an image each month and challenges writers to come up with fiction or poetry between 50 and 500 words long, which are then published online.

Look around you. 'Maybe you will see or hear something fun or unusual in the street or on the train, such as a person with a cumbersome parcel,' says Joanna. 'Ask yourself: What's in the parcel? Where are they going? Why is the person sitting on it? Why is it tied up with bright pink string? Use the incident and invent details.'

Have a way with words. Pick three words at random and weave them into a story.

Don't try to cover too much. 'Pick a particular incident or moment but don't give a verbatim account: turn it, twist it in some way,' says Joanna.

Flash fiction may be gaining in literary clout and popularity, but at six to 1,000 words its sheer brevity makes it one of the most accessible forms of writing for budding authors. Use the following pages to map out your own ideas and try writing your first piece of flash fiction.

Your ideas

....

....

....

....

....

....

....

....

....

....

....

....

Literary inspiration

Grab the closest book to you. Turn to page 18, read the fifth line down and make the next full sentence your starting point

Blank canvas

Take a few minutes to clear your mind. Close your eyes, breathe deeply and focus on nothing. Then write whatever comes into your head

....

....

....

....

....

....

....

....

....

....

....

....

....

....

....

....

....

....

....

....

....

....

....

By the clock

Set your timer, give yourself one hour and see what you come up with

....

....

....

....

....

....

....

....

....

....

....

....

....

....

....

....

....

....

....

....

....

....

Word search

Eccentricity. Rug. Deathbed.

Take these three words and tie them together in a story

....
....
....
....
....
....
....
....
....
....
....
....
....
....
....
....
....
....
....
....
....
....

In the bag

Imagine you've found a bag in the street. What is inside?
What do you learn about the bag and the person it belongs to?

....
....
....
....
....
....
....
....
....
....
....
....
....
....
....
....
....
....
....
....
....
....

Current affairs

Think of a news story you've read today, or an anecdote you have heard. Pick a person in that snippet and tell the tale from their point of view

....
....
....
....
....
....
....
....
....
....
....
....
....
....
....
....
....
....
....
....
....
....
....
....
....
....
....

Green is the colour of...

Use this as the start of your story

....

....

....

....

....

....

....

....

....

....

....

....

....

....

....

....

....

....

....

....

....

....

....

Ways to stay creative in a busy life

1 Out and about

People-watching can be a great inspiration. Conversations overheard on a bus could feed into your novels, someone else's clothes could prompt your next fashion design or the countryside outside the train window could be a future painting.

What do you notice?

....

....

....

....

....

....

2 Power lunch

Spend your lunch break drafting your novel, taking photographs around the area or sitting and sketching.

3 Surf's up

No time for a lunch break? Take 10 minutes to browse inspiring websites like Pinterest, Etsy or Instagram.

4 Screen time

Do you really need that much of it? Could you take half an hour out of your evening's social media browsing or TV viewing to work on your art?

5 Morning motivation

Weekend lie-ins can be heaven, and you can look forward to that date with your duvet all week long. Just once though, try setting your alarm clock early on a weekend morning, get up before everyone else and spend that quiet time with your art. You may find you achieve more than you expect.

6 **Culture vulture**
There is always more to learn from truly great artists. Visit an art gallery, unearth your Shakespeare or tune in to Radio 3 to catch up on some great classics, even if it's only for a few minutes.

7 **Social skills**
Meeting friends? Instead of heading for the pub, why not use this as an opportunity to be more creative? Start a knitting circle, a writing group or a book club and share your art with your friends.

8 **It's a way of life**
If your nine to five is really stopping you pursuing your dreams, could you change your life to give your art greater priority? Can you make money from your creativity, or could you cut down on household costs so you can work fewer hours and devote more time to your real love?

9 **Meditation station**
When it feels like everyday worries, chores and just general stuff are stifling your creativity, take time out to clear your mind. Spend 5, 10 or 20 minutes focusing on your breathing and allowing thoughts to come and go without overwhelming you. It could be the mental break that gets you unblocked.

10 **Dream catcher**
Some of the greatest artworks of all time came to their authors fully formed in dreams, like Samuel Taylor Coleridge's poem *Kubla Khan*.

Use this space to record inspiration that strikes after sleeping

Yoga for wellbeing

A simple yoga practice can connect your wellbeing to the world around you. Have you ever stopped to observe a tree? It stands tall and strong, rooted in the ground, surviving all seasons. Practising Vriksasana, or tree pose, helps you to stand equally as tall and strong. A grounding posture, it brings peace and calm to the mind and body, while lengthening the spine.

How to practise tree pose

Stand with your arms by your side – palms open and facing frontwards. Take a moment to breathe deeply, connect with your core and ground your feet with the earth below.

On an in-breath, bring your hands into prayer position at the centre of your chest. Take a few breaths, enjoying the peace and calm of this position.

Shift your weight onto your right foot. Imagine it has roots growing into the ground.

Slowly bend your left knee and then gently place the sole of your left foot against your right leg – you can use your hand to guide the foot. It can be along the inner thigh or the lower part of the leg, anywhere along the leg that feels comfortable, but never against the knee (this can cause injury). Some yogis place their foot with the toes resting on the floor and the sole against the right ankle.

On an out-breath, raise your palms in prayer position above your head. Take a few deep breaths in this position, with chest and shoulders open wide and legs strong and grounded.

Lower your arms back down to prayer pose in front of your chest, and lower your left foot back to standing position.

Take a moment to observe how your body feels. Now repeat the exercise on the other side of the body, grounding through your left leg and bringing the right foot to the left thigh. Practising tree pose on both sides will balance out the body. Stay grounded. You will soon be as strong, tall and majestic as a mighty oak.

Top tips

- If you feel a bit wobbly, open the arms wide to help maintain balance.
- To maintain focus, keep your eyes open and direct your gaze towards a fixed object directly ahead of you.

Conqueror's breath

Another simple but effective yoga exercise is Ujjayii pranayama, also know as conqueror's or ocean's breath. The practice of this breathing technique encourages the mind to become more focused, aids concentration and improves positivity. It generates internal heat and reduces respiratory problems, and can also help to reduce stress and anxiety.

How to practise conqueror's breath

1 *Sit in a seated position, tall and upright, straight spine, relaxed shoulders and face. Your eyes can be open or closed, whichever you find most comfortable.*

2 *Sit for a moment, breathing at your regular pace and allow your body and mind to relax.*

3 *Now take a deep breath in through your nose. As you exhale, round your mouth and flow the breath up along the throat and out through the mouth – just as you would breathe when fogging up a mirror, making a 'HA' sound.*

4 *Practise this breath flow for a couple of minutes and concentrate on feeling how the air travels through the throat and out through the mouth.*

5 *Once you're comfortable with this flow of breath, you're ready to do Ujjayii breathing. Close your mouth and repeat the breath flow described above, but this time when you come to exhale, do so through the nose. On the exhalation, you will observe a gentle ocean sound as the breath flows up along the curved back of the throat.*

6 *Try to keep the breathing ratio as one second on the inhalation and two seconds on the exhalation.*

For beginners, it's best to limit your practice of the Ujjayii breath flow technique – in through the nose and out through the nose – to no longer than five minutes. Observe how your mind and body feels afterwards.

Now, whenever you find yourself in a situation when you're feeling anxious and stressed, instead of letting it get the better of you, practise some Ujjayii breathing.

How does yoga affect your wellbeing? Use these pages to
note your different feelings after each simple yoga practice

....

....

....

....

....

....

....

....

....

....

....

....

....

....

....

....

....

....

....

....

....

....

....

....

Breathe

BREATHE is a trademark of Guild of Master Craftsman Publications Ltd

First published 2018 by
Ammonite Press
an imprint of Guild of Master Craftsman Publications Ltd
Castle Place, 166 High Street, Lewes, East Sussex BN7 1XU, United Kingdom

www.ammonitepress.com
www.breathemagazine.com

Compiled by Susie Duff
Editorial: Catherine Kielthy, Jane Roe
Words credits: Christine Boggis, Zoe Bowman, Jim Butler, Tracy Calder, Lorna Cowan, Liz Dobbs,
Juliana Kassianos, Nichola Ludlam-Raine, Lara Morgan, Dean Ratore, Gabrielle Treanor,
Renée van der Vloodt, Simone Scott, Carol Anne Strange, Dawattie Basdeo

Cover illustration: Sarah Wilkins
Illustrations and photographs: Shutterstock.com, Alamy.com, Getty.com,
Sara Thielker, Valesca Van Waveren, Laura Backeberg

ISBN 978-1-78145-469-5

Colour reproduction by GMC Reprographics
Printed and bound in China

AMMONITE
PRESS